GO ASL 422

PUBLIC SCHOOL 2
825 47th STREET
BROOKLYN 20, N. Y.

N D E A

N D E A

Your Telephone
and How It Works

Whittlesey House

McGRAW-HILL BOOK COMPANY, INC.

New York   London   Toronto

by

HERMAN SCHNEIDER IS SUPERVISOR OF SCIENCE
ELEMENTARY SCHOOLS OF NEW YORK CITY

YOUR
TELEPHONE
and how it works

HERMAN *and* NINA SCHNEIDER

pictures by JEANNE BENDICK

Also by Herman Schneider

EVERYDAY MACHINES AND HOW THEY WORK

EVERYDAY WEATHER AND HOW IT WORKS

YOUR TELEPHONE AND HOW IT WORKS

Copyright, 1952, by Herman and Nina Schneider and Jeanne Bendick. All rights in this book are reserved. It may not be used for dramatic, motion-, or talking-picture purposes without written authorization from the holder of these rights. Nor may the book or parts thereof be reproduced in any manner whatsoever without permission in writing, except in the case of brief quotations embodied in critical articles and reviews. For information, address Whittlesey House, 330 West 42d Street, New York 36, New York.

Published by Whittlesey House
A division of the McGraw-Hill Book Company, Inc.
Printed in the United States of America

Library of Congress Catalog Card Number: 52–7452

EIGHTH PRINTING

5544⁸

*To our children who sometimes
let us use the telephone*

*With cordial thanks to Mr. Karl
F. Steinhauer of Auto-
matic Electric Company
for valuable comments
on the first edition and
for suggestions adopted
in the second edition.*

Contents

People Like to Talk   9

Sound and Sound Makers   12

The Telephone   21

The Dial Telephone   56

Telephones That Travel   72

Index   95

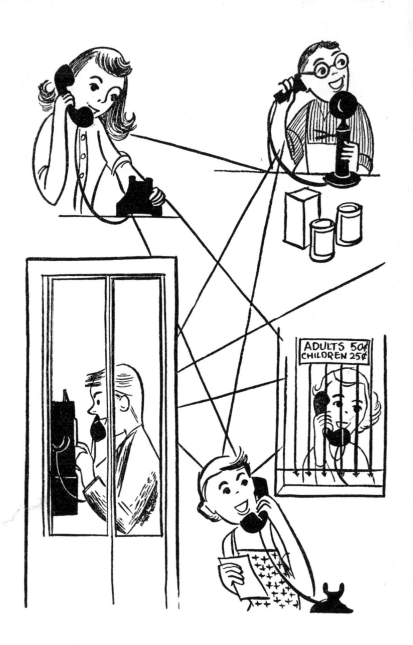

People Like to Talk

Pᴇᴏᴘʟᴇ ʟɪᴋᴇ to talk to each other, and they have all sorts of things to say—

What time does the movie begin?

Come to my party;

Send up six lamb chops and a pound of noodles;

I love you;

And lots of other messages.

It's easy enough to say things to somebody nearby, but when he's far away you have problems:

You can shout—but your shout travels only a short distance.

You can make a still

louder noise by banging a bass drum or shooting off a rifle—but you can't say very much that way.

You can build a signal fire—but you must have a clear space between you and the other person. There must be no buildings, mountains, or forests to block the way. And how would you use a signal fire to send a message such as: "No wonder our team lost today. They haven't got a single decent pitcher"?

You can send a letter— but you have to wait at least a day for an answer.

You can send a telegram—but even then you have to wait for an answer.

Or you can use a telephone.

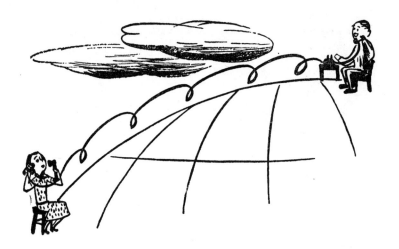

With a telephone you can talk to somebody at
the other end of town or the other end of the world.
You will be heard just as clearly as if the two of you
were in the same room. And you don't have to wait
for an answer, because the telephone can zip your
words from New York to Australia in less time than
it takes to blink an eyelash. How does a telephone
carry your words so quickly and clearly?

 It isn't hard to understand how a telephone
works, especially if you first understand a few things
about sound. So let's find out how sounds are made,
how they travel, and how they are heard.

Sound and Sound Makers

THE WORLD is full of sound makers, as you have found out when you tried to sleep late on a holiday morning. These sound makers come in all sizes and shapes, and are made of all kinds of materials. Some make pleasant sounds and some sound awful. But all of them make sound in the same way. You can find out what this is by doing a few simple things:

1. Touch two fingers to your Adam's apple and make a growling sound. Feel the buzzing movement in your finger tips.

2. Twang a stretched rubber band. Hear the sound made by the rubber band shaking rapidly back and forth.

3. Touch any sound maker—a bell, a radio, a piano, a drum—while it is making sound. Feel that same rapid shaking.

This rapid back-and-forth movement is called vibration.

VIBRATION

Anything that makes sound does so by shaking rapidly—vibrating. When you bang a drum you make the drumhead vibrate. When you strike the

keys of a piano, you cause strings to vibrate. When you speak or sing or growl, you cause two thin strips in your throat, called vocal cords, to vibrate. Every sound has its beginning in the vibration of something or other.

VIBRATIONS MUST TRAVEL

But vibration is only the beginning. Right at this moment a parrot in a South American jungle is screeching, a mother in China is singing to her baby, and somebody at the other end of your town is making dreadful sounds as he learns to play a cornet—but you can hear none of them. Before you can hear any sound, the vibrations must first reach your ear. How do vibrations travel to you?

HOW VIBRATIONS TRAVEL

Most vibrations reach you through the air. When any sound maker vibrates, it causes the air around it to vibrate, too. Above, below, and all around the vibrating sound maker, the air vibrates. These vibrations spread out rapidly in all directions. Wherever the air vibrates against something—the

walls, the ground, a tree—that something vibrates. And when the air around you vibrates, it causes your eardrums to vibrate. In your ears there are nerves that detect the vibrations and send signals to your brain. Then you hear sound.

VIBRATIONS GET WEAKER

Something happens to vibrations as they travel. They become weaker the farther they go. When somebody standing right next to you speaks, you can hear him well because the vibrations have only a short distance to travel. Only a small amount of air needs to be moved, so the full strength of the vibrations reaches your ears. But when he speaks to you from a great distance, a larger, heavier amount of air must be set into motion and the vibrations become weaker. You know that you can send a small toy truck whizzing across the floor with a flip of your finger, but a real truck can barely be budged by several strong men. The heavier a thing is, the harder it is to move—and this is true even of air.

In a way this is very fortunate. Think of what the world would be like if air vibrations continued to travel without becoming weaker and dying out. You would hear every sound made everywhere in the world, and what a din that would be!

HELPING VIBRATIONS

Sometimes, however, you want to talk to someone far away. Then you want the vibrations to travel far, and not to weaken quickly. You can help the vibrations in several ways.

One way is by speaking through a megaphone, or by using your cupped hands to make your voice louder, as a megaphone does. This sends most of the vibrations in one direction, instead of letting them scatter around. In this way, your voice can travel two or three times as far.

Another method is to aim your vibrations by sending them through a tube, so that all the vibrations travel to the listener. Perhaps you have tried this method by talking through a long piece of empty garden hose. If you did, you have found that even a whisper can be heard a hundred feet or more, which is quite a lot farther than the whisper would be heard without a tube to guide the vibrations.

SPEAKING TUBES

Can a tube, then, be used as a telephone for speaking over longer distances? It can, if the distances are not too great. Speaking tubes are used on some ships to enable the steersman high up in the pilot-house to speak to the engineer far below in the engine room. But a speaking tube would not do for talking across the distance of a mile or more, for two important reasons:

1. Even through a tube, the vibrations cannot just keep on going. The farther they go the more air must be set in motion and the weaker the vibrations become. Finally they die out entirely.

VIBRATIONS START OUT STRONG

))))))))))))

AND GET WEAKER AND WEAKER

2. Even if the vibrations remained at full strength all the way, a long tube would not be a good telephone, because most of the conversation through such a tube would consist of periods of silence. The longer the tube the longer the periods of silence. Let's see why.

SOUND IS SLOW

Sound vibrations take time to travel. Through the air they go a mile in about five seconds. That sounds fast, and it is fast, compared to the speed of a horse or car or most airplanes. But even at such a speed, it would take a whole minute for your words to travel through a twelve-mile tube, and another whole minute for the other person's voice to come back. In other words, after asking a question, you would have to wait two minutes for the answer. If you were talking through a tube that stretched across the whole country, you would have to wait eight hours! Such a conversation would be very boring.

FIRST YOU SEE HIM
HIT THE NAIL
THEN

YOU HEAR
HIM HIT IT

It may seem like a new idea to you that sound takes time to travel, but you have seen and heard it happen many times. When a carpenter is at work some distance away, say on a rooftop, you see him strike the nail and *then,* a little while later, you hear the bang. At a ball game, if you sit far

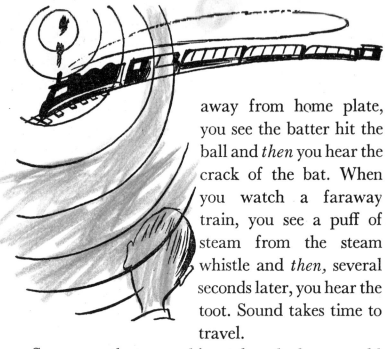

away from home plate, you see the batter hit the ball and *then* you hear the crack of the bat. When you watch a faraway train, you see a puff of steam from the steam whistle and *then,* several seconds later, you hear the toot. Sound takes time to travel.

So you see that a speaking-tube telephone would not be very good for long-distance conversations. The sound vibrations take too long to travel, and they become weaker and die out before they have traveled very far. We need to use something else in place of air—something that can carry vibrations much, much faster and much, much farther. That something is electricity.

Electricity in your telephone can carry your words, quick as a flash, to any part of the world. Let's see how your telephone works.

The Telephone

Now LET'S look at your telephone. Most likely it looks like this

Or it may be the kind that is fastened to the wall like this

It may be a coin telephone, like this

But no matter what shape it has, you can be sure of one thing about it; it has a cord coming out of it.

Inside the cord there are two copper wires, each one wrapped with cloth or rubber so that the wires cannot touch each other.

RUBBER
OR CLOTH WIRE CORD

If you could follow the two wires you would find that

They go out into the street,

Up above on telephone poles, or

Down below the street in cables,

JOE'S MARKET   CAKE

And continue on and on until they reach a building called the telephone exchange.

IN THE EXCHANGE

In the exchange there is a huge electric battery. Electricity flows out of this battery through the wires that come from your telephone. Inside the wires there is electricity. It flows through one of the wires all the way into your telephone and then out again through the other wire all the way back to the telephone exchange.

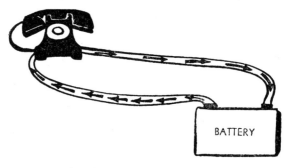

Into your telephone, through one wire and out through the other, the electricity runs smoothly and steadily—until you begin to speak. Then something special happens.

THE TRANSMITTER

The mouthpiece—the part you speak into—is shaped like a cup to catch all your voice vibrations. It is called a transmitter. To see what happens when

FRONT VIEW   SIDE VIEW

CARBON

you speak, we'll have to look inside the transmitter. There we find a little round box about as big across as a penny, but somewhat thicker. The box is filled with tiny black grains about the size of grains of sand. These are grains of black carbon, very much like bits of coal. Under a magnifying glass we can see that they have sharp edges and corners. The

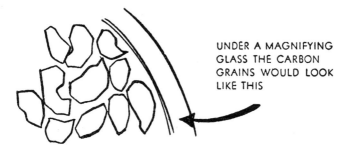

UNDER A MAGNIFYING GLASS THE CARBON GRAINS WOULD LOOK LIKE THIS

box contains thousands of these little black carbon grains, each one perfectly still, waiting for you to say, "Hello." Now let's see what happens inside the box when you start talking.

VIBRATIONS FROM YOUR VOICE

MAKE THE SIDES OF THE BOX VIBRATE

WHEN THE SIDES ARE PUSHED IN, THE CARBON GRAINS ARE SQUEEZED TOGETHER

WHEN THE SIDES MOVE OUT, THE GRAINS ARE "UNSQUEEZED"

WHEN YOU TALK

When you talk, your vocal cords vibrate, and this causes the air to vibrate, too. The air vibrations cause the sides of the little round box to vibrate in and out, in and out—one vibration of the box for each vibration of your vocal cords. Each time the sides of the box are pushed in, the carbon grains are squeezed together, like rubber balls in a box. Each time the sides move out, the grains are "unsqueezed." This squeezing and unsqueezing does something to the electricity flowing through the wires. To see what happens, let's look at how the wires are joined to the box.

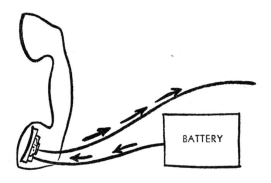

We find that one wire leads into one side of the box and the other wire leads into the opposite side. The electricity that came all the way from the telephone exchange through one wire, cannot go back without first flowing through the carbon grains. It *must* flow through them to get to the other wire that will take it back to the telephone exchange. Will the carbon grains allow the electricity to flow through?

They will and they won't, depending on what is happening to them. When they are squeezed, they touch each other snugly, side by side. They make a broad, solid path, and the electricity can flow easily through them.

But when they are un- squeezed, they touch only very lightly, and in many places not at all. Now the path is thin and broken, and the electricity has a hard time getting through.

In and out, in and out the grains move, squeezed and shaken by the vibrations of your voice. And each time they are squeezed together, the electricity flows well. Each time they shake apart, the electricity flows weakly.

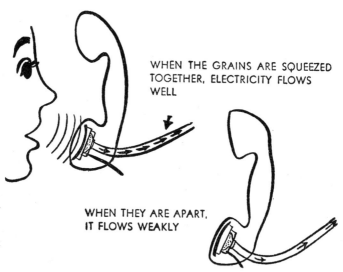

WHEN THE GRAINS ARE SQUEEZED TOGETHER, ELECTRICITY FLOWS WELL

WHEN THEY ARE APART, IT FLOWS WEAKLY

SPURTS

Before you started speaking, the carbon grains were loosely packed, and the electricity flowed in a weak but steady stream. But now it flows in "spurts," one spurt for each squeeze of the little box of carbon grains. And since those squeezes are caused by the vibrations of your voice, there is one spurt of electricity for each vibration. When you speak into a telephone, you chop up the steady flow of electricity into spurts—as many spurts as there are vibrations in your voice. Now the electric current is carrying the vibrations of your voice.

THE CURRENT FLOWS IN SPURTS

YOU CAN'T HEAR THE VIBRATIONS

So far, so good. Electricity is a much better carrier of vibrations than air, or water, or rock, or anything else you can think of. Electricity can carry the vibrations enormous distances with hardly any weakening. And it carries them at terrific speeds—

ELECTRICITY CAN TRAVEL
SEVEN TIMES AROUND
THE WORLD IN ONE
SECOND

a million miles in the time it takes you to count quickly from one to ten. That is, around the world seven times in a second! But there is one trouble with the vibrations carried by electricity—you can't hear them.

What good are vibrations that you can't hear? None at all. You can hold your ear close to a telephone wire and you won't hear a thing, even though two people may be chattering away at a great rate through that wire. Your ear has no way of hearing vibrations of electricity. The vibrations must first be changed into vibrations of air. Only these can reach your ear and be heard.

THE VIBRATIONS MUST BE CHANGED

The job of changing vibrations of electricity into vibrations of air is done by the part you hold to your ear. This part is called the receiver. Let's see how it works.

THE RECEIVER

A telephone receiver is quite simple. Its job is to change vibrations of electricity, which you can't hear, into vibrations of air which you can hear. To do this job, the receiver has two spools of wire and a thin disc made of iron. The spools of wire receive the electricity, and the disc causes the air to vibrate. Let's see how each part works, beginning with the spools of wire.

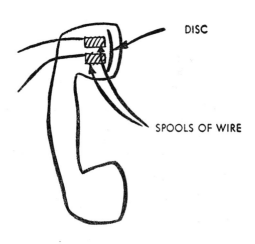

DISC

SPOOLS OF WIRE

THE SPOOLS

When electricity flows through a wire, something very interesting happens. The wire becomes a magnet. This happens in every wire through which electricity is flowing. Right now, if you're reading

ELECTRICITY RUNNING THROUGH A WIRE

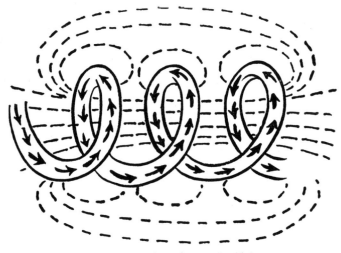

MAKES THE WIRES MAGNETIC

this by the light of an electric lamp, the wires of that lamp are magnets! You don't notice it because the magnetism is very weak, not enough to pick up even a tiny nail. But suppose you could take the magnetism from hundreds of feet of wire and crowd it into a tiny space. The magnetism in that space would be very strong.

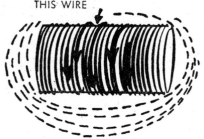

WHEN ELECTRICITY FLOWS THROUGH ALL THIS WIRE

THE MAGNETISM AROUND IT IS VERY STRONG

The spools of wire in a telephone receiver contain many feet of wire, all coiled up into a tiny space. When electricity flows through the wire, a very strong magnetism is set up. But when there is no electricity flowing, there is no magnetism.

THE PATH OF THE ELECTRICITY

The electricity in the spool of wire comes from the telephone exchange, but in a roundabout way. After leaving the telephone exchange, it flows through the carbon grains of somebody's telephone (the somebody with whom you are carrying on a telephone conversation) and then to the spools of wire in your receiver. The electricity, which started out as a steady flow, is chopped up into spurts by the vibrations of the somebody's voice, and each spurt then flows into your receiver.

THE MAGNET WORKS

As you have found out, a strong flow of electricity causes the spool of wire to become a strong magnet; while with weaker electricity the spool has practically no magnetism. So with each spurt of electricity, a spurt of magnetism is produced, one for each vibration of the speaker's voice. But you can't hear magnetism any better than you can hear electricity. We need something that actually makes the air vibrate. This is the job of the iron disc.

THE IRON DISC

Each time the spool becomes a magnet, it pulls the disc toward it. Each time the spool stops being a magnet, the disc springs back. The disc bends back and forth with each spurt of magnetism, and as it does so it causes the air in front of the disc to vibrate. The vibration of the air strikes your eardrum, and you hear the sound of the speaker's voice.

WHEN EACH SPOOL BECOMES A MAGNET IT PULLS THE DISC TOWARD IT

WHEN IT STOPS BEING A MAGNET, THE DISC SPRINGS BACK

BELL'S FIRST TELEPHONE

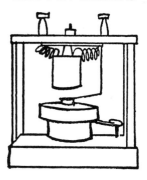

MAGNET

That's about all there is to an ordinary telephone receiver. Practically the same parts were used in the first telephone receiver invented in 1876 by Alexander Graham Bell. A modern receiver contains a few improvements that make it work better. One is a plastic-and-metal ring arrangement instead of the metal disc. Another is a small steel magnet that adds to the magnetism made by the spool of wire. Otherwise, most receivers are pretty much the same inside.

MORE RECEIVERS

Ordinary telephone receivers are built just large enough to fit your ear, but there are some that are as large as your head. You probably have such a large one in your house right now. The loud-speaker of a radio is really an oversized telephone receiver,

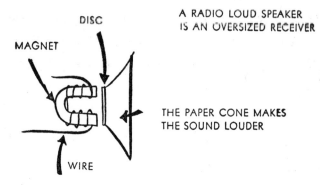

DISC

MAGNET

A RADIO LOUD SPEAKER
IS AN OVERSIZED RECEIVER

THE PAPER CONE MAKES
THE SOUND LOUDER

WIRE

with a few improvements of its own to make the sound louder.

Telephone receivers also come in very small sizes. The kinds used by partly deaf people are made tiny enough to fit into the ear, so that they can send all their vibrations directly inside where they can be heard better.

HEARING AIDS SEND
ALL THE VIBRATIONS
DIRECTLY INSIDE

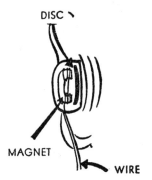

DISC

MAGNET

WIRE

THE TRANSMITTER AND RECEIVER WORK TOGETHER

You know now how the two parts of a telephone work. When you talk into a transmitter, sound vibrations cause a steady electric current to be chopped up into spurts of electricity, one spurt for each vibration. The electricity flows into the receiver of the person who is listening to you. In the receiving end of the telephone, it is changed into spurts of magnetism, and the magnetism makes an iron disc vibrate and produce sound. The listener receives your voice. So when you speak, air vibrations are changed to electrical vibrations that zip through wires to another telephone, where they are changed back again to air vibrations that are received by the person listening. When he speaks and you listen, the air vibrations go through the same changes from his transmitter to your receiver.

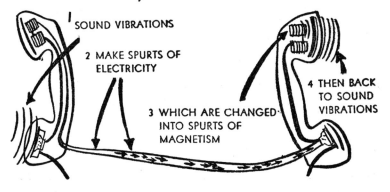

1 SOUND VIBRATIONS

2 MAKE SPURTS OF ELECTRICITY

3 WHICH ARE CHANGED INTO SPURTS OF MAGNETISM

4 THEN BACK TO SOUND VIBRATIONS

Now let's find out how your telephone is connected to the telephone of the person whom you are calling.

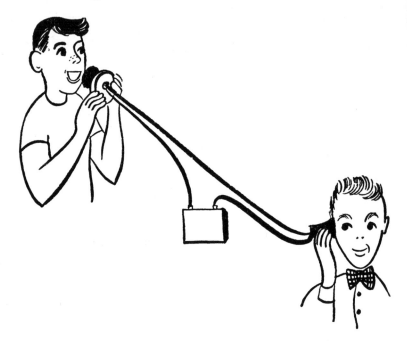

CALLING—JUST FOR TWO

Let's begin with the very simplest possible arrangement. Suppose you owned one transmitter and one receiver; you could join them as in the picture. A person at one end of the line could speak to someone at the other end, but the second person could not answer him. To have a back-and-forth conversation, you would need another transmitter and receiver, as in this picture.

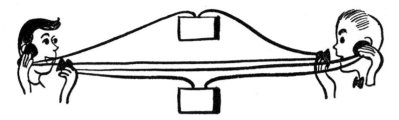

But such an arrangement calls for four wires between the two talkers. Wire is expensive, so if there is a way of using only two wires instead of four, we can save some money. And there is such a way. . . . We simply use the same two wires for both the transmitter and receiver, as the picture shows.

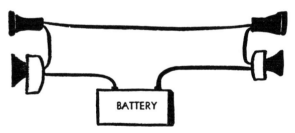

BATTERY

In this arrangement the electricity that flows through your transmitter also flows through your own receiver. When you speak to somebody, you also hear yourself. But there's nothing wrong with that, because you always hear yourself when you speak, with or without a telephone.

Now we're all set.

We can talk back and forth over the same two wires, and that's fine—for two people who care about nobody but each other.

CALLING ALL NUMBERS

Most people, however, want to have a choice. They want to be able to call their friends, make business arrangements, reach their doctor, find out about trains, and save themselves time and work in many ways. Most people want the telephone as a doorway to the world.

For such people we need an arrangement in which the wires from one telephone are not always joined to the wires from another, but only while they are talking to each other. Such an arrangement is called a switchboard. When you telephone to someone, the wires from your telephone are connected through a switchboard to the wires from the other telephone. Let's see how this is done.

MANUAL SWITCHBOARDS

Switchboards come in many sizes, from little ones the size of a portable radio to huge ones that fill an entire ten-story building. But there are only two main types—those that are operated by people and those that are operated by machinery. In the first kind you tell your number to an operator, while in the other you turn a dial.

Switchboards that are operated by people are called manual switchboards. Here's a picture of one. It looks rather complicated, but it isn't really. To see how it works, let's make a call from your telephone—whose number, let's say, is 5032—to your friend's, 9825.

WE BEGIN

We begin by lifting the telephone off its hook or base. When we do, a little light glows at the switchboard. This light is directly under a small hole called a jack. The jack has a number right next to it, 5032. This is the number of your telephone. There are many other jacks on the switchboard, each with its own little light.

Inside the jack there are two wires, and if you could follow them you would find that they go all the way through the town to one particular telephone—yours. The same is true of all the other jacks on the switchboard: each one has two wires that go to its particular telephone.

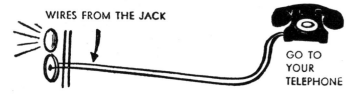

WIRES FROM THE JACK

GO TO YOUR TELEPHONE

NUMBER, PLEASE

Now the lamp under jack 5032 is lit, and that tells the operator that you want to make a call. To answer you, the operator picks up a pencil-shaped thing called a plug, and pushes it into jack 5032.

The light under the jack goes out and now the operator's telephone is connected to yours. She says, "Number, please." You tell her the number of your friend's telephone—9825. Let's see how the operator gets the number for you.

MAKING THE CONNECTION

To connect you to number 9825, the operator needs to join the wires in your jack—5032—to the wires in jack 9825, so that electricity can flow between your telephone and your friend's. However, part of the job has already been done. This is how. The plug that was pushed into your jack has a cord attached to it. Inside the cord are wires, and these wires end up in another plug. Now the operator simply picks up this other plug and pushes it into jack 9825.

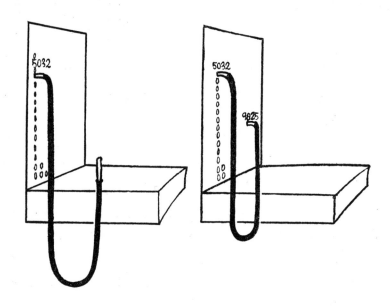

Now your wires are connected to the other telephone, and there is a complete roadway from your telephone to the other. But you can't talk to your friend yet because he doesn't know that you are calling him. He won't know until his telephone bell rings. To ring the bell, the operator presses a little switch called a ringing key.

HELLO

This allows electricity to flow through the wires to the bell, making it ring. When your friend answers, the ringing key is turned off and the conversation begins.

GOOD-BY

When you are through talking and hang up, a lamp next to the ringing key lights up, telling the operator you are finished. Then the operator pulls the plugs out of both jacks and the call is over.

As you can see, the chief job of a telephone switchboard and of the operator who works it is to join the wires coming from one telephone to the wires leading to another telephone. But there are other jobs to be done, and other machinery to do them. Let's look at some of these jobs and see how they are done.

COUNTING THE CALLS

One job is to count up the number of calls made from your telephone. In most cities you pay a certain amount for a call. In smaller towns and in the country you pay by the month, and can make as many local calls as you wish. In places where you pay by the call, there is a little counting machine attached from the wires of your telephone—a separate counting machine for each telephone. After you have made your call and hung up, the machine clicks off another call. Every month the number of calls is recorded, and the bill is sent to you.

COIN TELEPHONE

No bills are sent from coin telephones, because you pay for each call as you make it. With coin telephones you can't get the operator's attention just by lifting the receiver, because there is a little switch inside the telephone, like a lamp switch. This switch is turned on by the coin you drop into the slot. It causes the lamp at the switchboard to light up, telling the operator to plug into the jack above the lights. No coin, no light—and therefore no call.

QUARTER DIME NICKEL

MONEY BOX

COIN RETURN

A coin-box telephone has three slots—one for nickels, one for dimes, and one for quarters. It also has a device for telling the operator what coins you have dropped into the slots. This device consists of two bells—a little one that goes "ding" and a larger one that goes "bong." A nickel, falling through the nickel chute, causes the little bell to be struck once, making a single "ding" sound that the operator hears. A dime causes the same bell to be struck twice: "ding-ding." A quarter causes the larger bell to be struck once: "bong." And a coin dropped into the wrong slot doesn't fit the pocket and simply falls out into the coin return.

Of course, you don't want to pay for a call unless you have actually spoken to someone. If nobody answers, or if the line is busy, you want your money back; and coin telephones are equipped with a little device for returning it to you. The way it works is simple and interesting. When you drop a coin into the slot, it falls into a little pocket just above two chutes. One chute leads into the money box, to be collected by the telephone-company man who comes around regularly. The other chute leads to an opening marked "coin return."

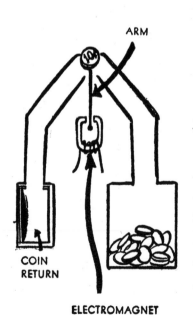

ARM

COIN
RETURN

ELECTROMAGNET

The coin stays above the two chutes until you hang up. If the call has gone through properly, that is, if someone at the other end has answered your ring, the coin is sent into the money box. This is done by a small arm that tips the coin into the money-box chute. The arm is operated by an electromagnet. This is a coil of wire that becomes a magnet when electricity

from the telephone exchange is sent through. If your call has not gone through and you hang up, electricity is sent through the coil from the opposite direction, causing the arm to be tipped the other way, into the coin-return chute. And you get your money back.

MORE OPERATORS

Let's go back to the telephone exchange, because all we've looked at so far is one switchboard and one operator, and there is much more to see. At the switchboard where your call was put through, you can see the jack with your number on it and the jack with your friend's number on it. There are many other jacks as well, each with its lamp above it— ten thousand jacks all together.

The wires from ten thousand telephones all lead to that one switchboard. The operator at that switchboard can connect any telephone of the ten thousand to any other. But isn't that an enormous number of telephones for one operator to tend? How can she take care of so many calls all by herself?

The answer is that she can't, and doesn't have to. Look around and you see twenty operators at twenty switchboards. Each switchboard looks exactly like the one that handled your call, with ten thousand jacks and lamps, and with the same numbers next

to each jack. You can find your number—5032—
at every switchboard, and also your friend's number
and every other number of the ten thousand. Your
call could have been handled by any one of the operators, because the wires from your telephone go
to every jack with the number 5032 on it.

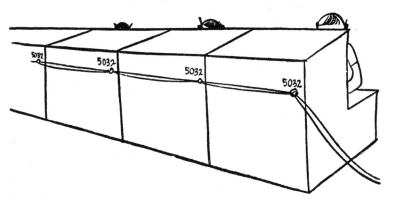

Well then, when you lifted the telephone to call your
friend, who decided which operator was to have the
honor of serving you? If every one of your jacks
(number 5032) had a lamp that lit up, all the operators would have answered your call. That never
happens, however, because only a few of your jacks
are equipped with lamps. Only the operators in
front of these lamps know that you want to make
a call. As soon as one of these operators plugs in,
the lights go out. This tells the other operators that
your call is being taken care of.

WHY TEN THOUSAND?

Perhaps you have wondered about the ten thousand telephones served at these switchboards. Why not twelve thousand, or fifteen thousand? The limit is ten thousand because of the length of the operator's arms. An ordinary person, with arms of ordinary length, can reach a certain distance to the right and left. Within that distance there is room for ten thousand jacks.

IN LARGER TOWNS

Many towns and cities have more than ten thousand telephones. Then the telephone company builds additional exchanges, one for each ten thousand telephones. Each exchange is given its own name, such as River, Townsend, and so on. Or the exchanges may be numbered—River 1, River 2, and so on. All these exchanges are connected by special telephone wires to each switchboard. When you telephone someone whose exchange is the same as yours, the operator simply connects your jack to the other one, and you can talk. For example, Townsend 1492 calling Townsend 2784 is this kind of simple call.

CALLING ANOTHER EXCHANGE

Suppose you call someone whose exchange is different. Townsend 1492 is calling River 8726. What happens?

When a call is made from one exchange to another, a special set of wires is used. In this call, the wires used are the ones that go from your Townsend exchange to the River exchange. When you ask for the number, your operator calls the River operator, who then connects you to River 8726. Each exchange in a town or city has special wires that go to every other exchange.

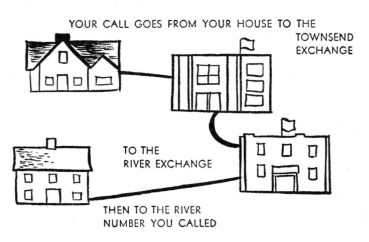

YOUR CALL GOES FROM YOUR HOUSE TO THE
TOWNSEND EXCHANGE

TO THE
RIVER EXCHANGE

THEN TO THE RIVER
NUMBER YOU CALLED

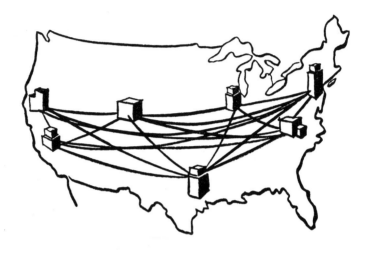

CALLING OTHER CITIES AND COUNTRIES

There are special wires from one city to another. These are called long-distance wires. When you want to make a long-distance call, your operator connects you with an operator at the long-distance switchboard. At this switchboard, the jacks have names instead of numbers—the names of the various cities to which she can connect you through the special long-distance wire. Through them you can speak to anyone at any other telephone in the country.

You can also speak to people in other countries, because there are long-distance wires from the United States to Canada and Mexico, and special overseas stations that carry your words by radio to receiving stations in other countries. Through these receiving stations you can be connected to almost any telephone anywhere in the world.

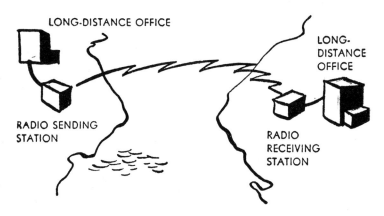

Passenger ships and transport planes are often equipped with ship-to-shore and air-to-land radio telephones. Even some trains and taxicabs are equipped with special telephones. You will find out how they work later on in this book, but first let's look into a different kind of exchange, one where machines do the work of a telephone operator.

The Dial Telephone

So FAR in this book, all the telephone connections have been made by a human being, a telephone operator. But you know that many jobs can be done more easily and quickly by machines than by human beings. When you lift your telephone to make a call through a manual switchboard—

The operator has to pick up a plug,

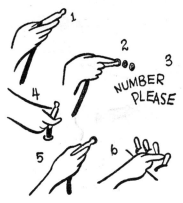

Place it in your jack,
Ask you what number
you are calling,
Pick up another plug,
Put it into the jack of
the called number,
And press a ringing key.
All these operations take
time and work. And if
your call is to a telephone in another exchange, still
more operations are needed that take still more
time and energy. But machines have been invented
that do the work instead of human beings. Such machines are being installed one after another in most
exchanges in this country.

THE EXCHANGE

An exchange where the connections are made by
machinery is called a machine exchange. If you
have visited one, you know it is quite a bewildering
place, full of clicking and buzzing machines. It
would take hundreds of books the size of this one to
explain the parts of every machine. But you can
have a pretty good idea by seeing how a call is made
on our own simplified machine.

First of all, let's keep in mind that any exchange,

whether manual or machine, has one main job to
do. An operator or a machine has the job of making
a connection—you might call it a bridge of wire—
between the wires from your telephone and the wires
to somebody else's.

You remember that in a manual exchange there
are one or more switchboards. At each switchboard
there are ten thousand holes called jacks. Inside
each jack is a pair of wires leading to one certain
telephone in town.

A machine exchange also contains switchboards
with wires leading to telephones, but the switchboards look different. Instead of having holes, they
have prongs sticking out. Each pair of prongs is connected, behind the switchboard, to a pair of wires
leading to a certain telephone. To make a connec-

tion for you, a machine must "build a bridge" of wire between your prongs and those of the person whom you are calling. Then electricity can flow between your telephone and the other person's, and the two of you can talk.

To see how this is done, let's follow a call step by step. Our own number, let's say, is 1201 (we won't worry about the name of the exchange at present) and we want to call 2376. To make the whole thing clearer, we'll watch each step first on a manual exchange, then on a simplified machine exchange.

LIFTING YOUR TELEPHONE OFF THE HOOK STARTS ELECTRICITY FLOWING

1. First you lift your telephone off the hook. This closes a little switch inside the telephone, allowing electricity to flow from a battery at the exchange, through one wire to your telephone, through the little switch, and through a second wire back to the exchange. In a manual exchange the electricity

causes a lamp to light under your jack, telling the operator that you want to make a call. In a machine exchange the electricity flows to your prongs and also to a part called a line finder, which will be explained soon.

2. In a manual exchange, an operator sees your lighted lamp, picks up a plug, and pushes it into the jack over the lamp. In doing so, the operator has "found your line." That is, she has started to build one side of a wire bridge—the side from you to somebody, but she doesn't yet know who the somebody is.

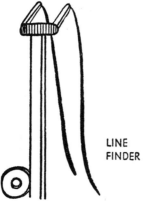

LINE FINDER

In a machine exchange, the line finder finds your pair of prongs. The line finder is a rod that can be moved up or down by an electric motor. At the top of the rod are two metal arms, each with a wire attached. The rod moves up until it finds your pair of prongs. How can it tell which prongs are yours?

The line finder can't see, but it can feel electricity. Your prongs have electricity in them, because when you lifted the phone you worked a switch that allowed electricity to flow. The electricity operates a little machine that stops the line finder when it has reached your prongs. The line finder, you remember, has two metal arms, each with a wire attached. The arms are now touching your prongs. That is, one side of a wire bridge has been built—the side from you to—whom? The machine doesn't yet know.

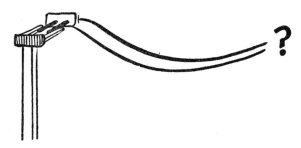

3. Next comes the "Number, please." In a manual exchange the operator says it. In a machine exchange a special kind of electricity is sent into your telephone, causing a humming sound called the dial tone. The dial tone is the machine's way of saying, "Number, please."

You tell the machine what number you want by turning a dial. The dial is a wheel with holes in it, through which you can see numbers. Let's see how it works.

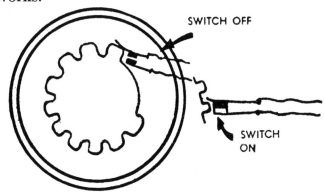

Under the dial, in the base of the telephone, is a wheel with ten teeth on it. This wheel is next to a small switch. When the wheel is turned the teeth bump the switch. Each tooth, as it turns past the switch, snaps it off and then on again. That is, if three teeth turn past the switch one after the other, electricity is turned off and on three times.

Now let's get along with our call. The humming dial tone tells us that the machine is asking, "Number, please." You want to call 2376, so you put your finger in the 2 hole, turn the dial, and let go. The dial snaps back, at the same time turning the ten-toothed wheel. As it turns, two of its teeth bump the switch one after the other, turning the electricity off and on twice. In other words, the steady flow of electricity between your phone and the exchange was interrupted. Two "shots" of electricity were sent through, and then the steady flow began again. When you dial the number 3, three shots of electricity are sent, then seven shots for the 7 and six for the 6. Now you have answered the machine's "Number, please." Let's see what happens at the exchange.

You know what happens at a manual exchange. The operator, after you tell her what number you want, completes the bridge of wire. She does this by picking up an "outgoing" plug, the wires of which are connected to your plug (the one she put into your jack). She puts this second, or outgoing, plug into the jack of the number you are calling.

With the bridge completed, electricity can flow between your telephone and the other. In a machine exchange the same job has to be done. Let's see how the machine does it.

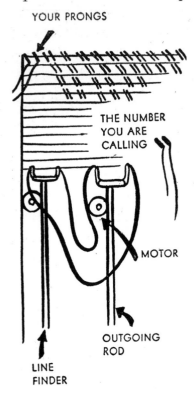

YOUR PRONGS

THE NUMBER
YOU ARE
CALLING

MOTOR

OUTGOING
ROD

LINE
FINDER

The machine has a second rod waiting, a partner to the line-finder rod. Let's name this one the "outgoing rod." This rod has two metal arms on top just like those on the line-finder rod. Attached to the arms of the outgoing rod are the ends of two wires—the wires that come from the line finder. The outgoing rod is ready to carry these wires to the pair of prongs that we ask for when we dial 2376. Let's find those prongs on the machine's switchboard.

When we study the switchboard closely, we find that the prongs are arranged in rows. There are one hundred rows, one above the other, and one hundred pairs of prongs in each row. The number we want —2376—is in the twenty-third row, and it is the seventy-sixth pair of prongs in that row. Watch the outgoing rod get it for us.

When we dial the first two numbers of our call
—23—the rod, moved by a motor, moves up to row
23. When we dial the next two numbers—76—the
rod moves across the row to the seventy-sixth pair of
prongs. Now the bridge is complete, with a pair of
wires running between the prongs of 2376 and our
own.

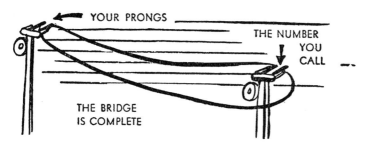

The connection has been made, and now the machine sends a special current of electricity to ring
the other person's telephone bell. As soon as he picks
up the receiver, we can start talking.

It took a long time to describe the operation of
our simplified machine, and it would take much
longer to describe the real machine in a telephone
exchange. But it doesn't take more than a few seconds for the machine to do its work. Most of the calls
are completed, and the called telephone is ringing,
within two or three seconds after you have finished
dialing.

Perhaps you have wondered about how our simplified machine is different from a real machine exchange. A real machine, which is actually many machines working together, has many more jobs to do besides connecting you to another telephone. Here are just a few of the jobs:

1. If the called telephone is busy, the machine sends a special buzzbuzz of electricity—the busy signal.

2. If nobody answers the called telephone's ringing after several minutes, the machine connects you to an operator, who tells you the connection cannot be made. You hang up. Otherwise a person might dial a number, be called away from the phone and forget about his call. The other phone would ring and ring and drive the neighbors crazy.

3. If you dial a number for which there is no telephone, or the number of a person who has recently canceled his telephone service, the machine connects you to an operator who tells you about it.

4. In cities where you pay according to the number of calls, the machine adds up each call on a special little adding machine attached to your line. It adds up only the calls actually completed, not those that gave you a busy signal, or those where nobody answered your ring, or calls to the telephone company's office. The machine also times your calls, clicking off one call for each three min-

utcs that you usc the phone. This is a modern example of the old saying that "time is money."

5. If you are calling from a coin-box telephone and nobody answers or the line is busy, the machine sends a "coin return" current of electricity when you hang up.

6. In towns and cities with more than one telephone exchange, the machine must first connect you to the right exchange, where another machine connects you to the called number. Each exchange has its own number, which you dial first. For example, dialing 32-6655 will first get you exchange number 32 and then telephone number 6655 in that exchange.

However, it's rather difficult to remember a long string of numbers, so the various exchanges may be given letters instead. In place of number 2, the letters A, B, or C are used. These three letters are all in the number 2 hole in the dial, while in place of 3, the letters D, E, or F are used, and so on for the rest of the alphabet. It's easier to remember DArling 6655 than 32-6655.

7. You may remember that in a manual exchange there are usually many switchboards and many operators. The wires from your telephone are connected to one jack at each switchboard. A spe-

cial machine feeds your call to an operator who is not busy at the moment. The same thing is true in a machine exchange. There are many machines that can connect you to the number you are calling. A special "selector" picks a machine that is not busy with another call.

8. In some cities you can find out about the weather by dialing a special number. When you do, you hear the pleasant voice of an operator saying something like this: "Fair and warmer this afternoon, followed by showers and clearing tonight. Present temperature 67 degrees . . ." and lots more. Don't bother to thank the operator, for she won't hear you. She spoke the words into a machine that made a record of them; and the record will be played over and over again until the weather bureau sends in a new report to be recorded and played.

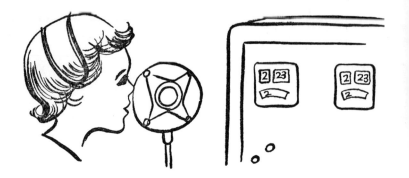

9. In some cities you can dial a special number and get the correct time. This information is given by an operator who has the fascinating job of speaking into a transmitter, saying: "When you hear the signal the time will be 8:31 and one-quarter . . . beep . . . when you hear the signal the time will be 8:31 and one-half . . . beep . . . when you hear . . ." you guess the rest. The "beep" sound comes from a machine controlled by a very, very accurate clock. The operator comes from a family of very patient people who are not easily bored.

And there are other machines that do still other jobs. Right now, for example, machines are being installed in many exchanges to enable you to dial long-distance calls without first having to tell your number to a long-distance operator. Other machines have been invented, and in the future you may see some of them in operation.

One interesting machine makes the telephone into a two-way television affair. You and your friend can see each other as you speak, or the grocer can show you the selection of melons on sale that day.

But before we get too far into the special telephones of the future, let's look at some special telephones of today. Let's look at the telephones that travel.

Telephones That Travel

So far, you have learned about telephones that stay put. The telephone in your home stays put on a desk in the living room, on a shelf in the kitchen, or some other place where you can always find it. And so does the telephone of the person whom you call. Most of the telephones of the world are the "stay put" kind.

But there are also telephones that go traveling. You have probably seen police cars equipped so that the driver can talk with police headquarters or with other police cars. Perhaps the taxicabs in your town have the same sort of traveling telephone. Most airplanes are equipped with telephones for keeping in touch with the control tower at the airport, or for permitting passengers to make calls or receive calls while the plane is in flight. You can even make a call from a ship at sea, from a train in motion, or from a submarine undersea. In the air, on land, at sea, and undersea—the traveling telephone can work anywhere.

But how does the traveling telephone work? There are no wires to join it to others, and yet the conversations go flashing back and forth, from land to air and from ship to shore, just as quickly as if the wires were there. What carries the words so quickly, and why can't we hear them buzzing around us? You can find out the main ideas by taking them one step at a time.

First, let's look at the very simplest kind of ordinary telephone connection. Here it is.

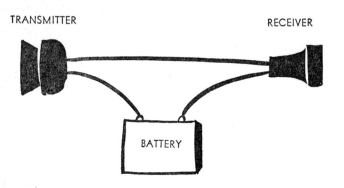

TRANSMITTER　　　　　　　　　RECEIVER

BATTERY

Notice that we have:

　A transmitter into which you speak,
　A receiver to listen to,
　A battery to furnish the electricity,
　And wires to carry it.

When you speak into the transmitter, the vibrations of your voice chop up the electricity into spurts, one spurt for each vibration of your voice. The spurts of electricity cause the iron disc in the receiver to vibrate, making sounds that can be heard by the person at the receiver. Nothing special so far; this is just like the telephone you have learned about before.

Now let's make this into a traveling telephone, one in which there are no wires joining the transmitter and the receiver. We'll begin by doing a curious thing—we'll snip two wires across the middle. Then we'll join the cut ends, like this.

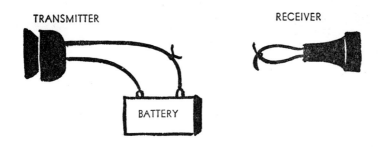

This is a strange state of affairs. Now there is no connection between the transmitter and the receiver. Now when you talk into the transmitter, the spurts of electricity just race around through the wire to the battery. They don't get to the receiver at all, because the wires are not connected to the receiver. What good is this?

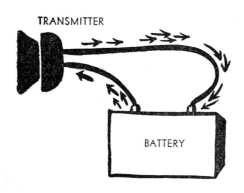

Lots of good, as you'll see in a moment.

Whenever electricity flows through anything, it sets up magnetism around that thing. Those spurts of electricity that go racing through the wires set up spurts of magnetism around the wires. The spurts

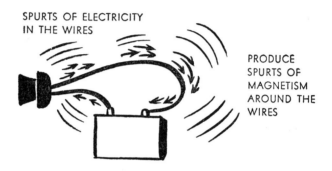

SPURTS OF ELECTRICITY
IN THE WIRES

PRODUCE
SPURTS OF
MAGNETISM
AROUND THE
WIRES

of magnetism—one for each vibration of your voice —go zipping out in all directions at an enormous speed. In less than a tenth of a second they cover the entire world.

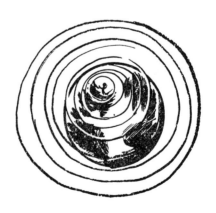

If these spurts of magnetism can be changed into spurts of electricity, they can be used to operate a telephone receiver. Then the receiver will change the electricity into sound. So we need to find some arrangement that will change magnetism into electricity. We don't have to look far, because the arrangement is already there. The wires at the receiver do the job for us. This is how.

Whenever magnetism flows across a metal, it causes electricity to start flowing through that metal. The wires at the receiver are made of a metal

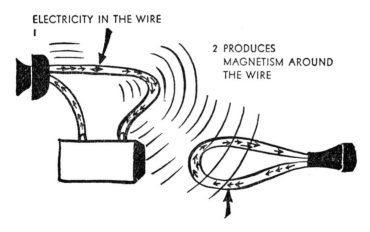

ELECTRICITY IN THE WIRE

2 PRODUCES MAGNETISM AROUND THE WIRE

3 WHICH PRODUCES MORE ELECTRICITY IN THE WIRES OF THE RECEIVER

copper. The magnetism from the transmitter wires—one spurt of magnetism for each vibration of your voice—causes spurts of electricity to flow through the receiver wires. The electricity causes the iron disc in the receiver to vibrate, and sound is made.

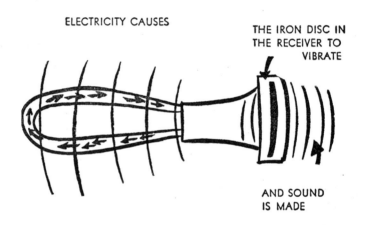

ELECTRICITY CAUSES

THE IRON DISC IN
THE RECEIVER TO
VIBRATE

AND SOUND
IS MADE

That's good, isn't it? That seems to be what we started out to do. We started out to make a traveling telephone, one in which there were no wires between the speaker and the listener. And this arrangement seems to be the answer, because there are no wires between the two. However, let's not start any celebrations just yet. There is still a problem to be solved.

The problem is this. This magnetism can make only weak electricity, too weak to make a sound loud enough to be heard on any telephone. What good is a sound if you can't hear it? No good at all. If we are to hear the sound, we need strong electricity.

We have no way of strengthening the weak electricity. We can't feed it vitamins and build up its muscles. But we can do something else. We can use the weak electricity to work a delicate switch. This switch can turn on and off a stronger electricity. This stronger electricity is obtained from a battery connected to the receiver.

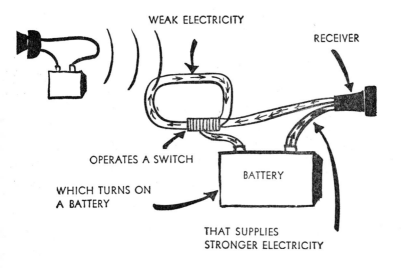

WEAK ELECTRICITY

RECEIVER

OPERATES A SWITCH

WHICH TURNS ON
A BATTERY

BATTERY

THAT SUPPLIES
STRONGER ELECTRICITY

In this way, the weak spurts of electricity set up by the speaker's voice will turn the switch on and off, once for each vibration of the speaker's voice. Each "on and off" of the switch will allow one spurt of the strong electricity to flow through the receiver and make one strong sound vibration.

There are two kinds of switches that can do this job. One kind is called a vacuum tube, or just tube for short. The other kind is called a transistor. Transistors are a fairly new invention, but they are simpler to understand, so we'll look at them first.

A transistor is a little piece of a special kind of metal about the size of a match head. Connected to the piece of metal are wires that bring in the current that was too weak to make a sound you can hear. Also connected to the piece of metal are

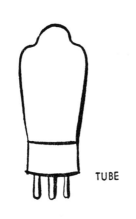

TUBE

TRANSISTOR

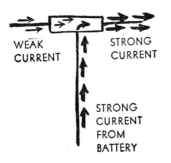

WEAK CURRENT

STRONG CURRENT

STRONG CURRENT FROM BATTERY

wires from a strong battery. The metal itself acts as the switch.

When the weak electricity flows, the metal turns on the strong electricity. This strong electricity flows through the wires into the receiver and makes a good loud sound which you can hear.

A tube is more compli-cated, but it does the same job. A weak current flow-ing into the tube switches on a strong current, which causes the receiver to make a sound you can hear.

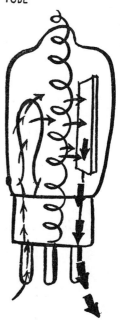

WEAK CURRENT FLOWING INTO THE TUBE

Each spurt of mag-netism sweeping in from the faraway telephone speaker makes a weak spurt of electricity. The weak electricity flows through the transistor or tube. These switches turn on the strong electricity and send it, spurt by spurt, into the receiver that makes the sound.

SWITCHES ON STRONGER CURRENT

Although traveling telephones come in many sizes and shapes, they all work in the same way. Now that you know some of the main ideas of how they work, we can make a list of the things that happen when two people talk to each other over a pair of traveling telephones.

Let's say that Officer Brown in Patrol Car 5 is talking with Officer Smith in Patrol Car 9.

1. Officer Brown speaks into a telephone transmitter. His vocal cords vibrate and cause the air to vibrate.

2. The vibrating air causes the carbon grains in the transmitter to be pressed together and then shaken apart. Together and apart, together and apart, one shake for each vibration that Officer Brown's vocal cords make.

3. The shaking of the carbon grains causes a steady electric current to be chopped up into spurts of electricity.

4. Each spurt of electricity produces a spurt of magnetism.

5. The spurts of magnetism go zipping out of a metal rod that is fastened to the outside of Patrol Car 5.

6. After they leave the metal rod, the spurts of magnetism spread out quickly in every direction.

7. As they spread out, they bump against another metal rod. This rod is attached to Patrol Car 9.

8. As they strike the rod, they cause very weak spurts of electricity to flow through the rod.

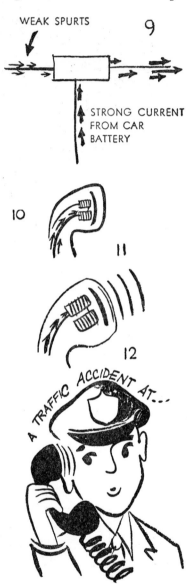

WEAK SPURTS

9

STRONG CURRENT
FROM CAR
BATTERY

10

11

12

A TRAFFIC ACCIDENT AT...

9. The weak spurts of electricity flow into transistors or tubes. The transistors or tubes are switches. Each spurt causes the switch to turn on and off, once, a strong electric current from the car battery.

10. The spurts of strong electricity flow into a telephone receiver.

11. In the receiver, the spurts of electricity are changed into spurts of magnetism that shake an iron disc back and forth.

12. The shaking of the iron disc causes the air to vibrate.

13. The vibrating air causes Officer Smith's eardrum to vibrate and then he hears sounds: "A traffic accident on Pine Street."

Quite a number of things happen when Officer Brown speaks to Officer Smith. They happen very fast, in much less time than the wink of an eye. And the same things happen when Officer Smith speaks to Officer Brown. Each patrol car has the same parts in its traveling telephone. Each car has one set of parts for speaking and another set for hearing the other fellow speak. And the same is true of other kinds of traveling telephones. But before we find out about these other kinds, let's clear up two questions that may have occurred to you as you were reading about the two police cars.

1. How do the spurts of magnetism from Officer Brown's car find their way to Officer Smith's car?

The answer is, they don't find their way. They just spread out in every direction, all over the world. Wherever they bump against anything made of

metal, they cause a weak electric current to flow through the metal. Right at this moment there are weak electric currents flowing through metal things all around you—the radiators in your room, the coins in your pockets, even the gold and silver fillings in your teeth (if you have fillings). Of course, you needn't feel alarmed, because the electric currents are very, very weak. They could be a million times as strong and still you wouldn't feel them. But the weak electric currents are there, strong enough for the tube or transistor to "feel" them.

2. Why doesn't the rod on Officer Smith's telephone pick up all the conversations from all the traveling telephones in the world?

Actually, it does. But the rod is connected to a special part called a tuner. This tuner acts like a keyhole. You know that you can't push any key into any keyhole, because the two must have the same shape if one is to fit into the other. The spurts of magnetism that come out of Officer Brown's car have first been "shaped" by a special part. The tuner in Officer Smith's car is built to allow these spurts to come through, but it stops others of a different shape.

Let's look at one of these tuners. This is what it looks like from the inside.

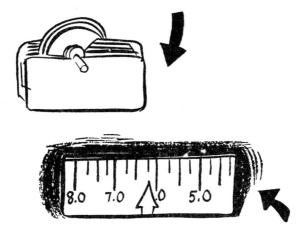

And this is what it looks like from the outside.

It looks like a radio dial, doesn't it? That's because it *is* a radio dial! A radio is really the receiving part of a traveling telephone. The transmitting part, the part that sends out words and music, is the broadcasting station. The microphone at the station is really a telephone transmitter, while the loudspeaker in your radio is a large telephone receiver.

The tubes in your radio work in exactly the same

way as the tubes in Officer Smith's traveling tele-phone. So in learning about traveling telephones you have also learned something about radio as well. This is bargain day, two for the price of one.

Now let's look at some other traveling telephones. We'll begin with the smallest, which is hardly bigger than a cigar box. It's called a handy-talkie, a very good name for it because it's certainly handy in emergencies. Soldiers use it in places where it is not practical to string up telephone wires. Firemen have handy-talkies for keeping in touch with each other inside a burning building, for reporting to their officers outside, and for receiving instructions. Here's a picture of one.

You know what the rod on top does. It receives the spurts of magnetism coming from the other

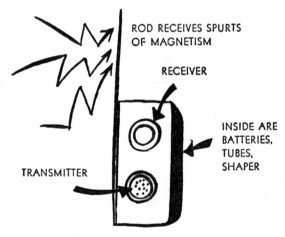

ROD RECEIVES SPURTS
OF MAGNETISM

RECEIVER

INSIDE ARE
BATTERIES,
TUBES,
SHAPER

TRANSMITTER

telephone, and it also sends out the spurts of magnetism from inside. The telephone transmitter and receiver are on the front of the box. Inside there are batteries to supply the electricity for talking and hearing. There are also transistors or tubes to act as delicate switches for turning the battery current on and off, a "shaper" that gives a special form to the spurts of magnetism going out, and a tuner that lets in only spurts of the right shape.

Handy-talkies are small and light, but they are not very powerful. They can be used over a short distance—a mile or so. For longer distances a larger, more powerful kind is used, called a walkie-talkie. It has heavier, more powerful batteries, and

more tubes and transistors, but it works in the same way as the handy-talkie.

Here is a still bigger and more powerful traveling telephone. It is used on airplanes for keeping in touch with the control-tower operators at airports along

the way, and with the pilots of other airplanes. There is no rod for receiving and sending the messages. Instead there is an antenna—a wire attached to the top of the plane. This wire is longer than a rod, and it can pick up a fainter message from a fairly long distance. For still longer distances, the pilot reels out a long wire that trails way behind the plane. With the wire out, and with a powerful traveling telephone in his plane, the pilot can carry on a conversation with somebody thousands of miles away.

The most powerful traveling telephones are the ones used on ships. Here there is no problem of weight, as there is on an airplane. The batteries can be tremendous and powerful, the other parts can be as big and heavy as is necessary, and the antenna is a really long one that stretches all the way from one mast of the ship to the other. Through such a powerful telephone you can talk with someone on another ship halfway around the world!

Ship-to-shore conversations are an easy matter, too. Special shore telephone exchanges are equipped to receive and send messages this way. Through these exchanges you can call a passenger on a ship, or he can call you, in hardly more time than it takes to dial a call to your friend down the street. Your conversation travels part of the way by wire—from your telephone to the exchange—and the rest of the way through the air—from the exchange to the ship. Your words travel through the wires as spurts of electricity, and through the air as spurts of magnetism, yet they can travel halfway around the world in less than a tenth of a second.

Traveling telephones go almost everywhere. Some businessmen have telephones in their cars, to keep in touch with the office. They can call the office (or any other telephone) while driving along the highway. And they can receive calls just as well.

There are traveling telephones on some trains, too. On these trains you can be connected to any other telephone, just as in your own home. The conversation is carried by radio waves to a special railroad exchange, and by wire from there to the other person.

THIS TRAIN TELEPHONE IS CONNECTED THROUGH
THE WHEELS AND THE TRACKS TO AN EXCHANGE

At sea, on land, in the air—traveling telephones can work for you anywhere.

And there are still other machines, equally marvelous and clever, doing their part of the work swiftly and surely. But even more marvelous and clever than all these machines are the thousands of people who made those machines possible. Scientists, engineers, and technicians worked for many years to invent and design and improve each separate part of these complicated machines.

But the important thing about any machine is not that it is marvelous and complicated or that many intelligent and skillful people invented it. The really important thing is that all this intelligence and skill is used in making life more pleasant and safe for all of us. With a telephone near, the world is near, too. Your family and friends, your doctor, your neighbors, all are brought closer to you. With a telephone nearby, no one need ever feel alone.

INDEX

Air, vibrations in, 14-16
  (*See also* Sound)
Airplanes, telephones on, 90-91

Battery in telephone exchange, 24
Bell, Alexander Graham, 35
Bells, ringing of, 45
Busy signal, 66

Cables, 22-23
Calls, counting of, 45-46, 67
  long-distance, 54-55
  in machine exchanges, 59-65
  on manual switchboards, 41-45, 59-60
  not answered, 66
  overseas, 55
  timing of, 67-68
  wire connections in, 38-40
Carbon grains in transmitter, 25-29
Coin-box telephones, 46-49, 68

Connections, within exchanges, 52-53
  in machine exchanges, 58-65
  on manual switchboards, 43-45
  from one exchange to another, 53-54, 68
  in traveling telephones, 74-81
  by wires, 38-41
Cords, 21
  on switchboards, 43-44
Counting of calls, 45-46, 67

Dial telephones, calls on, 59-65
  weather and time information, 69-70
  working of dial, 62-63
Dial tone, 61-62
Disc in receiver, 31, 34

Electric lamp, magnetized wires in, 32
Electricity, in receiver, 32-34

Electricity, in transmitter, 26-30
  in traveling telephones, 74-81
  vibrations in, 29-30
    changed to sound, 30-31, 34, 37
Exchanges, 23-24
  calls from one to another, 53-54, 68
  connections within, 52-53
  machine, 56-70
    connections in, 58-65
    special jobs of, 66-70
  manual, 41-45, 49-52

Handy-talkies, 88-89
Hearing aids, 36

Jacks in switchboards, 42-45

Light, electric, magnetized wires in, 32
Line finder in machine exchanges, 60-61
Long-distance calls, 54-55
Loud-speakers, 35-36

Machine exchanges (*see* Exchanges, machine)
Magnetism in traveling telephones, 76-81
Magnetized wires, 32-34
Megaphones, 17
Mouthpieces, 24-28

Operators, work of, 43-45, 49-52, 56-57
Outgoing rod in machine exchanges, 64-65
Overseas calls, 55

Plugs in switchboards, 43-45
Police patrol cars, telephones in, 82-88

Radio in traveling telephones, 87
Radio loud-speakers, 35-36
Railroad trains, telephones on, 93
Receivers, 31-35
  working with transmitters, 37

Ships, telephones on, 91-92
Sound, electric vibrations changed to, 30-31, 34, 37
  production of, 12-13
  speed of, 19-20

Speaking tubes, 17-20
Spools of wire in receiver, 31-34
Spurts of electricity, 29, 34, 74-75
Switchboards, jacks in, 42-45
  in machine exchanges, 58-65
  manual, 41-45
    with many operators, 49-52
  plugs in, 43-45
  purpose of, 40-41

Telephone calls (*see* Calls)
Telephone exchanges (*see* Exchanges)
Telephone poles, 22-23
Telephones, future improvements in, 70-71
  invention of, 35
  traveling (*see* Traveling telephones)
  types of, 21
Television by telephone, 71
Time information service, 70
Timing of calls, 67-68
Trains, telephones on, 93
Transistors, 80-81
Transmitters, 24-28
  working with receivers, 37
Traveling telephones, 72-73
  description of, 82-88
  kinds of, 88-94
  working principles of, 74-81
Tubes, speaking, 17-20
  vacuum, 80-81
Tuners in traveling telephones, 86-87

Vacuum tubes, 80-81
Vibrations, 13-14
  in electric current, 29-30
    changed to sound, 30-31, 34, 37
  speed of, 19-20
  in transmitter, 26-30
  traveling, through air, 14-16
    through tubes, 17-20

Walkie-talkies, 89-90
Weather information service, 69
Wires, 21-23
  magnetized, 32-34
  in receivers, 31-34
  in switchboards, 42, 44
  telephones connected by, 38-41
  in transmitters, 26-27